Deadly
POISON
DART FROGS

by Jennifer Dussling

Consultant: Gabrielle Sachs
Zoo Educator

BEARPORT
PUBLISHING

NEW YORK, NEW YORK

Credits

Cover, © Chris Mattison/age fotostock/SuperStock; TOC, © John Arnold/Shutterstock; 4, © Mark Smith/Photo Researchers/ Photolibrary; 5, © Jürgen Müller/imagebroker/Alamy; 6A, © Mark Moffett/Minden Pictures/Getty Images; 6B, © Craig K Lorenz/ Photo Researchers/Photolibrary; 6C, © blickwinkel/Kaufung/Alamy; 6D, © Michael Pitts/Nature Picture Library; 7, © Brian Kenney/Oxford Scientific/Photolibrary; 8, © Mark Moffett/Minden Pictures/Getty Images; 9, © Petra Wegner/Alamy; 11, © George Grall/National Geographic/Getty Images; 12, © Dr. Morley Read/Shutterstock; 13, © Rauschenbach/Mauritius Images; 14, © Derek Brown/dbimages/Alamy; 15, © Mark Moffett/Minden Pictures/Getty Images; 16, © Albert Lleal/Minden Pictures; 17, © Neil Bromhall/Nature Picture Library; 18, © Michael & Patricia Fogden/Minden Pictures/Getty Images; 19, © Michael & Patricia Fogden/Minden Pictures/Getty Images; 20-21, © Jim Zuckerman/Corbis; 22, © Dave Watts/Alamy; 23TL, © Mark Moffett/Minden Pictures/Getty Images; 23TR, © Dr. Morley Read/Shutterstock; 23BL, © Mark Moffett/Minden Pictures/Getty Images; 23BR, © Pete Oxford/Nature Picture Library; 24, © Eric Isselée/Shutterstock.

Publisher: Kenn Goin
Senior Editor: Lisa Wiseman
Creative Director: Spencer Brinker
Design: Becky Munich
Photo Researcher: Sakshi Saluja./S. Kripa; Q2AMedia

Library of Congress Cataloging-in-Publication Data

Dussling, Jennifer.
 Deadly poison dart frogs / by Jennifer Dussling.
     p. cm. — (Gross-out defenses)
 Includes bibliographical references and index.
 ISBN-13: 978-1-59716-720-8 (library binding)
 ISBN-10: 1-59716-720-7 (library binding)
 1. Dendrobatidae—Juvenile literature. I. Title.

 QL668.E233D87 2009
 597.87'7—dc22

                    2008011905

For more information, write to Bearport Publishing Company, Inc., 101 Fifth Avenue, Suite 6R, New York, New York 10003. Printed in the United States of America.

10 9 8 7 6 5 4 3 2

Contents

Frog Power!

In the hot, steamy **rain forest**, a hairy **tarantula** spots its dinner.

It's a tiny, bright yellow frog, sitting on the ground.

The frog is no match for the tarantula . . . or is it?

The tarantula bites the frog.

Suddenly, the spider starts foaming at the mouth.

Then its heart stops and the spider dies.

What happened?

The frog was poisonous!

tarantula

Pretty Frogs

Poison dart frogs come in many beautiful colors.

They can be green and black or yellow with black stripes.

Others are bright blue or red all over.

One kind is orange with black spots.

They may be cute, but don't touch them!

Many poison dart frogs have fun nicknames. A strawberry poison dart frog is often called "blue jeans" because it looks as if it's wearing a pair of jeans.

A Bright Warning

A poison dart frog's bright colors are a warning that tells other animals "Stay away!"

If an animal eats the frog and lives, it remembers how sick the frog made it.

It knows how yucky it tasted.

The bright colors remind the animal to look for a different kind of meal in the future!

Poison dart frogs
may be deadly, but they're
also tiny. The biggest ones
are about three inches (8 cm)
long! One of the smallest
kinds, nicknamed "buzzers,"
are only about three-quarters
of an inch (2 cm) long!

9

Poison Pores

When facing an enemy, poison dart frogs get nervous.

To protect themselves, poison oozes from **pores** in their skin.

Some frogs are more poisonous than others.

Eating certain types of these animals will make an enemy sick, while eating other kinds can cause death.

Some frogs are so poisonous that it's not even safe to touch them!

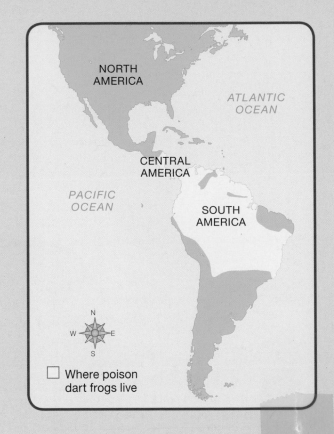

NORTH AMERICA

ATLANTIC OCEAN

CENTRAL AMERICA

PACIFIC OCEAN

SOUTH AMERICA

N
W E
S

☐ Where poison dart frogs live

Poison dart frogs live in the rain forests of Central America and South America.

Deadly Insects

What makes these pretty frogs poisonous?

Scientists don't know for sure.

They think the poison comes from certain types of insects, such as ants or beetles, that the frogs eat.

In fact, poison dart frogs born in a scientist's lab or at the zoo aren't poisonous at all.

The reason is that they don't eat the same food as frogs in the wild.

ants

Hunting Darts

At times, the frog's poison comes in handy for people.

Some hunters in Colombia, South America, use the frogs to help them get food.

They rub the tips of their darts in the poison found on the frogs' backs.

Then they use a blowgun to shoot the darts at animals.

The poison is strong enough to kill birds, monkeys, and even jaguars!

dart

Tadpoles

Poison dart frogs aren't poisonous when they're first born.

Some types of female frogs, such as strawberry poison dart frogs, lay their eggs on the damp ground.

When the eggs hatch, the babies, called **tadpoles**, are legless and have long tails.

They can't live on the rain forest floor.

They need to be in a place that has lots of water.

Where do they go?

strawberry poison dart frog eggs

Mother poison dart frogs lay between 2 and 30 eggs. Some mothers and fathers will pee on the eggs to keep them wet.

A Perfect Home

The best place for tadpoles to live is in treetops!

The father or mother frog climbs a plant with a tadpole on its back.

The parent looks for thick waxy leaves that catch and hold rain.

The tadpole will be gently placed into the rain-filled cup.

There is plenty of water and food here for the baby.

tadpole

Only one tadpole
goes into each cup.
An enemy may find
one little creature,
but it won't find
them all!

19

Growing Up

After a few weeks, a tadpole's body changes.

It grows legs, and its tail shrinks.

It becomes an adult frog.

Now it can catch its own food to eat.

Anyone looking to feed on it had better WATCH OUT!

A poison dart frog can live for as long as 15 years!

Another Deadly Defense

A fire salamander's bright colors send the same message as a poison dart frog—*Stay away!* The bold yellow markings on its head, back, and tail are a warning. If an animal attacks a fire salamander, the salamander squirts poison from pores on its back. The poison can fly as far as six feet (2 m)! It burns the eyes and mouth of the enemy and tastes really bad, too. Next time, the animal will know that yellow and black mean "Watch out!"

Glossary

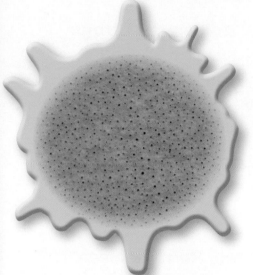

pores
(PORZ)
tiny holes in a
person's or
animal's skin

rain forest
(RAYN FOR-ist)
a warm place where
many trees grow
and lots of rain falls

tadpoles
(TAD-*polez*)
baby frogs

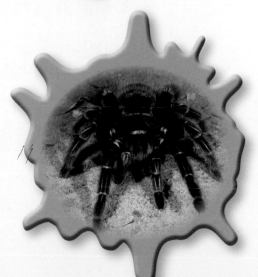

tarantula
(tuh-RAN-chuh-luh)
a big hairy spider

Index

Read More

Clarke, Dr. Barry. *Amphibian.* New York: Dorling Kindersley (2000).

Dewey, Jennifer Owings. *Poison Dart Frogs.* Honesdale, PA: Boyds Mills Press (1998).

Fridell, Ron. *The Search for Poison Dart Frogs.* New York: Franklin Watts (2002).

Learn More Online

To learn more about poison dart frogs, visit
www.bearportpublishing.com/GrossOutDefenses

About the Author

Jennifer Dussling, a longtime fan of poison dart frogs, has been eager to write a book about her favorite amphibians for many years. She's the author of several other nonfiction books for kids, including *Stars, Pink Snow and Other Weird Weather,* and *Slinky, Scaly Snakes.* She lives in Huntington, New York, a town that, as far as she knows, has no poisonous frogs.